MEN, WOMEN, AND GHOSTS

ALSO BY DEBORA GREGER

Movable Islands (1980)
And (1985)
The 1002nd Night (1990)
Off-Season at the Edge of the World (1994)
Desert Fathers, Uranium Daughters (1996)
God (2001)
Western Art (2004)

MEN, WOMEN, AND GHOSTS

DEBORA GREGER

PENGUIN POETS

PENGUIN BOOKS

Published by the Penguin Group

Penguin Group (USA) Inc., 375 Hudson Street, New York, New York 10014, U.S.A.
Penguin Group (Canada), 90 Eglinton Avenue East, Suite 700, Toronto, Ontario,
Canada M4P 2Y3 (a division of Pearson Penguin Canada Inc.)
Penguin Books Ltd, 80 Strand, London WC2R 0RL, England
Penguin Ireland, 25 St Stephen's Green, Dublin 2, Ireland
(a division of Penguin Books Ltd)
Penguin Group (Australia), 250 Camberwell Road, Camberwell,
Victoria 3124, Australia (a division of Pearson Australia Group Pty Ltd)
Penguin Books India Pvt Ltd, 11 Community Centre, Panchsheel Park,
New Delhi - 110 017, India
Penguin Group (NZ), 67 Apollo Drive, Rosedale, North Shore 0632, New Zealand
(a division of Pearson New Zealand Ltd)
Penguin Books (South Africa) (Pty) Ltd, 24 Sturdee Avenue, Rosebank,
Johannesburg 2196, South Africa

Penguin Books Ltd, Registered Offices:
80 Strand, London WC2R 0RL, England

First published in Penguin Books 2008

1 3 5 7 9 10 8 6 4 2

Copyright © Debora Greger, 2008
All rights reserved

Pages 105 and 106 constitute an extension of this copyright page.

LIBRARY OF CONGRESS CATALOGING IN PUBLICATION DATA
Greger, Debora, 1949–
Men, women, and ghosts / Debora Greger.
p. cm.—(Penguin poets)
ISBN 978-0-14-311444-4
I. Title.
PS3557.R42M46 2008
811'.54—dc22   2008003520

Printed in the United States of America
Set in Adobe Garamond and Bliss
Designed by Sabrina Bowers

*for Jean Justice
and in memory of Donald Justice*

*for Deborah Kaplan
and in memory of Roy Rosenzweig*

CONTENTS

IV

V

I am standing in a church-yard
alone. Everywhere the heather gleams
as far as the eye can see. For whom am I waiting?
A friend. And why does he not come? He is already here.

—TOMAS TRANSTRÖMER

MEN, WOMEN, AND GHOSTS

I

When I began, I was like the others; I believed that two canvases, one for gray and one for sunny weather, would be enough.

—CLAUDE MONET

HORACE

I. Odes 1.14

O ship, a ground swell threatens
to set you adrift—look out!
Hurry to reach the harbor—no, don't stop
to look, but you've lost your oars.

The mast has snapped. Sails slap at the wind.
Your hull needs rope to tie it back together.
Canvas has torn, but you no longer
have gods to get you out of trouble.

Though you're built of the best pine
from the most noble forest, upon a plank
of which your famous name is lettered—
and so beautifully—who can trust paint?

You make a sailor nervous. Be careful,
or you'll become a toy of the storm.
You who, not that long ago, were just
my headache, my pain in the neck,

but who now have my heart aboard,
steer clear of those narrow seas
that cut past the bright lights
marking the rocks of the Cyclades.

II. Odes 2.36

With incense, and some music,
and a sacrificial calf, let's thank the gods
who watched over N_____. He's safely home
from the far West, bringing kisses

for all his old friends, especially L_____,
his first, his oldest pal. How many years ago
did they have the same teacher?
They put on their first long togas together.

Don't forget to mark this day in red
on the calendar, or to show your devotion
to a jug of wine. Don't stop the wild dancing,
the kind they do down in S_____.

When it comes to the drinking contests,
don't let B_____ be outdrunk
by the not-so-dumb D_____.
And don't forget roses, and parsley—

which lasts—and lilies, which don't.
Let everyone swoon over D_____,
but she won't leave her new lover.
She'll be all over him like ivy.

AFTER HORACE

I. To the Fifties

Some poets, Horace says, spend their lives
going over the same old ground: some suburb
      of love. A parking lot
      at the shopping mall of loss.

My river, wind-hammered into a silver tray,
bears a tumbleweed past the nuclear plant.
      Past my parents' house,
      my heart has turned to dust.

I am five again, what have I done to myself?
The doctor setting my broken wrist on Sunday
      was the county coroner.
      Over the helium balloon,

a shiny green snake he'd given me for being good,
he told my mother why he was late:
      a boy's body had been fished
      from an irrigation canal.

Who was that boy? Who remembers him? Taller,
the cottonwoods still whisper there, faint syllables,
      the breath of a breeze.
      Once I lashed the leaves,

sweetly sappy, into a wreath that threatened
to come apart before anyone was crowned.
      I raise a leaf to the lost, I send it
      downriver, a heart-shaped boat.

II. To the Sixties

Puget Sound

O ship, no waves would take you back to sea,
and there was nothing you could do: you made
       for port but ran aground
       near Point No Point. As if

to skirt the driftwood guarding the cliff, you rode
a sandbar at a tilt. You rode the kelp,
       fair weather and fog. Moonlight,
       man-made, spilled from a porthole

into a pool of rust. Someone loved you.
Someone hung out laundry in semaphore,
       calling you home. Oh,
       for a life so unbalanced!

Later, my disillusion, but for now,
President Kennedy was on his way
       to my hometown, to open
       the newest reactor. How far

to November 1963? Ship
south of Deception Pass, do you rust in peace
       by waters older than the coldest war?
       History would clamber aboard.

III. To the Seventies

With incense, and rock music, and the beef,
corn-fed, of Iowa, I would give thanks, love,
        for your return from the east.
        Go on—return the kisses

of old housemates and the college friend
just passing through, sporting the tie-dyed T-shirt
        of the Ivy League—was it
        a teacher or a joint you shared?

Down at the Deadwood, let there be no limit
to the cheap drinks. Don't stop the seventies' dances.
        Let your old girlfriend outdrink
        some other aspiring poet.

Let me mark the morning after you drove all night,
Long Island to Iowa. Here are roses, cut
        from paper, and celery,
        stuffed in a drinking glass.

I looked out the window. A wall made beautiful
by ivy, weakened everywhere it clung.
        Was it last week I was someone else's?
        How long till you slept with another?

IV. To the Eighties

Enough! So the gods sent snow to Rome?
Invited to dine with enemy or friend, good Romans
       brought a sack of the stuff
       to chill the wine.

So what did we bring to the Eternal City?
Your pocket picked, we watched the yellow Tiber,
       its broad back empty,
       the present lying in ruins

about us. We walked the way tourists walk
through history, nose in a guidebook to the dust.
       If some Roman bought a Vespa
       with your credit card,

we didn't know that yet. In a church that seemed
to grow out of a temple, we stood, barbarians
       too late to do anything
       but note a Roman column

sliced like a carrot to decorate the floor.
I saw a ceiling bossed with New World gold
       and did not pray under it.
       At the Protestant Cemetery,

outside the old city, I saw a bus pull up.
From it poured French teenagers who stood
       in a ragged, giggly line
       so each one could peek

through a chink in the wall—at what?
They seemed unchanged by whatever they saw.
       I took my place behind them
       and, through an eyehole

the size of a picture postcard, saw the grave
of the young Keats. What was it to them,
that stone carved in English
for *one whose name was writ in water*?

V. To the Nineties

Florida

O my subtropical students! Don't you want wings
of your own? Wings barely flapping, I'd drift
     out of the classroom and lift
     like a vulture toward the interstate,

looking for lunch. Late afternoon would find me
in the next county, roosting in a cypress
     up to its knees in the Styx.
     The skin on my ankle would roughen.

It reddened. I was feathered at the elbow.
Which poetic voice was mine? The raptorious moan
     of a schoolgirl dragging a line
     of yours into her own language,

blushing furiously, cursing you under her breath.
Dear Horace, I would pick your bones so clean,
     cleaner than your critics.
     What more could you ask?

VI. To the Double Oughts

Was Spain rattling its spears? And what of Scythia?
Don't ask me, dead Roman. Forget foreign affairs.
      In the New World, I thought
      we were guarded by an ocean.

Up the East Coast, a smooth-cheeked tide receded,
the sand left ashen. A sea-rose shook.
      The blade of a moon sharpened
      while we slept in early September.

Our cost of living rose in taller and taller towers,
but don't worry. I had simple needs. I liked things big.
      Love no longer wore us out
      at night. There's nothing to see—

go back to your own stony bed, old Quinctius,
under the umbrella pine. Let the wine god
      shoo away the wolves
      who worry your grave.

There's no longer a slave to mix springwater
with wine gone vinegar. Lie down next to the bones
      of that woman Horace called easy.
      He used her name to shame her

and made her immortal instead. Where is her hair,
once done like a long-dead Spartan girl's,
      in the very latest style?
      Tell me her lyre survived.

II

The sealed vessels—between which there could be no communication—of separate afternoons.

—MARCEL PROUST

TAXI TO STONEHENGE

I passed a window full of televisions
        as gray as British bankers,
                though imported.
        And there in England I saw
the twin towers of its former colony
        crumble like toys made of fire
                and brimstone,
        the enormity of it more
terrible, reduced to fit a living room.

Were we the only Americans in Bath
        that November? So insisted
                the taxi driver
        winding his way to Stonehenge.
And there stood the stones just over a rise—
        as if just yesterday, back
                in the Iron Age,
        some first farmer had tried
to clear a field so he could plant it.

And there they still sat as if, over the hill,
        would come a last wagon,
                two centuries late,
        and men to complain how hard
to break off a piece they could carry away.
        For what earthly use was this folly
                in the eighteenth century?
        There were great houses to be built.
The newly rich lived lives made sweeter

by ships full of trinkets bound for the Gold Coast
        and then, with human cargo,
                for the New World.
        Bales of cotton staggered
onto Bristol dock—O sprigged muslin-to-be,

O spring frocks! Jane Austen,
           does your ghost
     ever range this far from Bath
on its walks? If so, I apologize.

I wore last year's coat. It wasn't enough
        that chilly British morning.
                   But the stones
           were dressed in lichen even older.
We walked the circle of path that kept the henge
           safe from our touch.
                   We walked it again.
        How many had died
to leave the stones standing there?

LETTER TWO HUNDRED YEARS LATE

Dear J. A.,
Your father's bones have been moved
to a hillside plot with a better view,
as if, down the street, he might still see
his tall, thin daughter, not so much in a rush
to buy quill and ink as to miss nothing.
Whose gown is news of the empire's latest frills?

And then you've hurried past the years
when a woman might marry. In a muslin dress
no longer the latest style, and no proper coat,
only a shawl—stout coats for women
undreamed of yet—you near the Assembly Rooms.

Who assembles there now? A quartet saws at old airs
behind closed doors. The basement is crowded
with mannequins—have you slipped in
to the costume museum, where no one ever goes?
Tell me how that pair of dancing slippers,
held together by embroidered flowers,
could last a single night. Were they never worn?

In more sensible shoes, you've vanished
into the second distance so beloved
of gardeners, painters, and young ladies
too refined to have anywhere else to go
one afternoon but out past the present
into the ground mist of memory.

Remember how sun loved the stone
that built Bath? The sun didn't know
how beautiful it was until it hit a wall—
the architect was right. In the Pump Room,
the young waiter knew he was beautiful enough
not to have to taste the waters.

But I wasn't. Rain from the Mendip Hills
in the Mesolithic—so that's what I drank.
It tasted ancient, alchemical:
a fallen leaf gone black with rot,
transmuted to diamond under pressure—
enough dancing lessons, and a girl might become
wife of some firstborn, landed male.

You don't need to take the waters—
you're immortal. Your books no longer insist
they're just "by a lady"; they bear your name
into the classrooms of England.
In her thrift stores, they come to rest.

I have a pair of embroidery scissors
for you, shaped like a crane:
the long beak snips, seeming to feed.
Your fingers in the handles make the bird's feet,
though its wings stay folded forever.

NAGASAKI, 1600

after Rai Sanyo

Past the bay, along a seam in the silk
where sea and sky meet, a dot appeared,

and then spread as if a seamstress,
feeling two pieces threaten to ripple apart,

had pricked her finger. A red sun rose in the west,
and the lookout ordered the cannon fired.

At the guard posts, archers unwrapped their bows.
And a cry ran the streets like a pack of dogs.

The red-haired men were tall, their ships even taller.
There was not enough wind to fill the great sails.

The anchor was big enough to keep our whole world
from floating off. They shouted at it

as if loudness would make them understood.
The heart of the barbarian—it was difficult to plumb.

Our small boats went to meet their giant tortoise shell,
lest it run aground in our shallows.

The emperor asked the court poet why the strangers had come.
A tall ship, he said, was just a leaf lost on the ocean,

an ocean embroidered, wave by silvery wave,
across a kimono. Like ants worked in gold,

sailors clung to the leaf. What was there to fear from them?

BRIGHTON, 1877

The town is famous for beauty,
by which the natives mean a building

wears a cap shaped like an onion
and perches on stilts above the ocean.

I, secretary to the first Chinese ambassador
to Lun-dun, have seen it with my own eyes.

Men of taste, tiring perhaps of the sport
or repose that brought them here

from the capital, have hollowed their way
into the cliff, to a chamber nearly the size

of their dancing rooms. And there, in glass tanks,
they have placed fish as foreign to these parts as I,

but still in their native garb. I have seen no gowns
as beautiful as those ruffles, spots, and stripes

that can only circle back to where they started.
Yes, I have come to know a Viennese waltz

when one passes before my eyes. For myself,
I wobble along the pretty wooden bridge

that goes nowhere but up in air, then out to sea.
Thus a wanderer may lean and look—at nothing, really.

And so one arrives at the music pavilion,
a lesser onion. When I am back in court

in Lun-dun, wearing the color of western mourning
as decreed by their empress, I shall think

of a brocaded fish brought from afar.
It bowed and scraped against the glass.

Let them think I honor her dead consort.

HER POSTHUMOUS LIFE

How long is this posthumous life of mine to last?
—KEATS TO HIS DOCTOR, ROME, 1820

I remember where I am,
for the light of London enters the room,
grimy as a chimney sweep.

He is here, too, in the corner
he has taken for his own, just a shade
in the shadow of the curtains.

He whispers his name,
which was to have been mine as well,
and I find myself possessed

of that lost girlishness
he claimed would slay him. But did Death call
at Wentworth Place?

No, Death booked passage
from Gravesend to Naples, then shared a carriage
on the Roman road.

What am I to a dead poet?
I am saddled with what never was, stooped
as a man of the docks

who straps to his back
the saddlebags of memory, making of himself
a beast of burden.

I am easily distracted.
He spies on me in mirrors. In shop windows,
in the days when I still went out.

Children, I am too old
for the latest fashions, though your father—
the wine merchant's clerk—

does not know I am
his elder by a dozen years. Before I was your age,
I knew a young man

who abandoned the study
of medicine to write poetry instead,
some of it to me.

I thought little of it
at the time, but you will have heard his name.
The world does not know mine.

He may have taken my letters,
unopened, to the grave, but here are his to me.
You are not to show them

to your father, who knows nothing
of this, either; but they will be of some value
after I am gone.

Do I worship the dead?
One need scarcely exchange a word with them.
He matches my footsteps.

Who knows how long
I have nursed this ghost? In a moth-eaten redingote
long out of style,

he dictates to me
his latest, an ode. I do not like it, though
I do not appear.

To Darkness, it begins,
and then goes on. Goes on into darkness,
knowing the weight of earth.

ON STOREY'S WAY

I.

This is the hour
an owl would head home to sleep
through the dawn chorus that followed,

blackbird and thrush
singing their tiny hearts out
philosophically, *Teach me! Teach me*

I see a tree!
What is a tree? Why
is there no brown light like me?

But first a cry broke
in two, cut off by a call.
The door of dream drew back

from a story
with nowhere to start.
It started—*think back a breath*—

with a screech
tearing day from dark.
A field mouse taken by an owl?

Nailed to the wall
of the garden for its own protection,
a rose laid open a blood-purple blossom.

II.

Down Storey's Way I walked,
out of my old life,
into the cemetery.

At the tomb of Wittgenstein I stood:
a slab with his name and dates
bore no other words;

but someone had laid a pinecone
and a penny there, on one
of the few graves

not overgrown. Grief was abandoned
to its own devices, yet
over the wall,

green wood burned near Storey's End.
To this, his doctor's house,
he came to die.

From the upper room might he have seen
this cemetery tree
and heard

a blackbird phrase and rephrase
a last treatise on color,
the color of smoke?

If a ghost appeared, it could glow,
but if it looked gray,
how would we paint it?

FAUNA BRITANNICA

I. The Bank Vole

Giant hogweed blooms by the ditch,
      like a street lamp,
      a poisonous parasol
over a tiny beaten path. Vole,
      you run the banks
      of England like a clerk,
made late by counting seed, more seed.
      Rich in salvage,
      your bank grows:
a moorhen has docked, unloading
      a drinking straw,
      a candy wrapper.
On a beer can crushed and stuck
      in the rushes
      she means to nest.
But you, rat, where are you,
      the stray cat asks.
      Just to be safe,
you tunnel under the cow parsley,
      a burglar escaping
      back into the bank.
New weed builds over the old,
      over your vaults.
      In a single summer
rises all of western civilization
      on waste ground,
      ragwort and yellow flag
bright as new coin for a week or two.

II. The Green Woodpecker

Bird, you're far too bright
    to be believed,
    let alone British.
Red crown, black mustache,
    green back,
    yellow rump—
don't I know you from a book,
    you fashion plate?
    Edwardian dandy,
self-taught scholar of male plumage,
    twelve-inch body
    just a footnote
to the sticky six-inch tongue—
    out of old woods
    on the new edge
of Cambridge you venture to feed.
    On college lawn—
    aren't you the soul
of Frazer, once of Trinity Great Court,
    now of the graveyard
    that town edges toward?
For doesn't the soul pass into a bird,
    just as he noted
    the Malays believed?
For, to a bough that catches fire
    in the late sun,
    you lift, startled aloft—
I have come upon you on his grave.
    The gates of hell
    have rusted open.
The river to the underworld is just gravel,
    the ferryman gone,
    a golden bough

no longer gold enough to take us
    down to the dead
    and light our way back.

THE GIANT OCTOPUS OF PUGET SOUND

That evening, the talk was all of sex—
not why her husband wasn't home,
which was never mentioned,

but how the old Pole, her guest of honor,
just back from Seattle, had seen
the giant octopus mate.

You ordered specimens like a meal,
he said. You waited
the days it took

the divers to return from the Sound.
At last your glass tank cleared,
you still waiting to see

the world's longest spermatophore
leave one of his tentacles
and enter her oviduct. Slowly,

a chair was brought for the professor
of reproduction (retired).
I forgot to ask

if, for an octopus, ink came before sex.
Of the higher animals present
that very English evening,

he is dead and she is divorced.
Those still together—
you and I—

read each other like old books,
the pages best left uncut.
Ink, spilled ink!

LETTER FOUR HUNDRED YEARS LATE

Dear W. S.,
With goat hair and straw,
they have rebuilt your Globe:
on the bank of the Thames it squats,

so clean you wouldn't recognize it.
And from the New World we come
to see men, mincing in dresses,
speak in the voices of mice.

Was that your ghost we saw force its way
through a thicket of chairs
to catch a drift of thistledown
that fell from a false ceiling of real sky?

The man who played the queen
dragged you along with her train.
You bumped into a pillar, then into a fool.
Over that "O" left open to the elements,

a jet wormed its way to Heathrow,
drowning him out. Like actors, afternoon shadows
took their time to fall. When, at last,
the last dead man had been applauded,

were you the shade who trailed us
down to the Underground? Across the tracks,
a rat made entrance through velvet grime,
dressed for the evening in the finest soot.

A small dark thing with a plague to its name,
it did not flinch at the steely scream
of a train making its entrance late.

THE COAST OF BOHEMIA

Thou art perfect, then, our ship hath touch'd upon
The deserts of Bohemia?

—WILLIAM SHAKESPEARE,
The Winter's Tale

Four flights up,
the strange sea creatures of Bohemia
waited to be combed

by any beachcomber who took a wrong turn
on the bank of the Thames.
High above mud that Shakespeare must have known,

there they were, made of glass
and kept in glass cases. Even if I didn't move,
the finest filaments

of lamp-work quivered as if we were underwater.
A sea slug held its breath.
A medusa shook out its tangled hair.

That man who crossed the Atlantic,
then went back home, and his son, who went as far
as the Adriatic—

was there any creature they hadn't attempted
to render in melted sand?
Stiffly they'd sat for the latest that science had to offer:

a studio photograph.
They held the pose as if they were preserved
as specimens, these men who

worked not from life but from someone else's drawings.
　　　　They got a few spots wrong,
these men who look like hermit crabs

　　　　　in the woolen suits
they buttoned themselves into, layer by layer.
　　　　These men made necklaces

of the finest paste. They sold glass eyes
　　　　　to taxidermists.
An anemone shuddered and drew me in.

　　　　Common moon jellyfish,
what tore at the moorings of my heart?
　　　　The room swam with salt

as if some great glass ship had passed over us.
　　　　　As if a young man
not yet become my great-grandfather

　　　　had booked passage
from Bohemia for some place he'd never seen:
　　　　　a landlocked sea

called Nebraska, glassy with prairie grass.

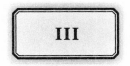

III

Did I not once *have a pleasant, heroic, legendary youth to be written on leaves of gold—I was too lucky!*

—JULES LAFORGUE

TO THE WEST

In the library of a foreign town, homesick
for something to call home, I sat down
with the *Encyclopedia of the American West.*

O sagebrush! O tumbleweed!
Though I had walked an English garden—
had stalked past a New World passionflower—

I was still yours, who were never mine to take.
The swaybacked roofs of Cambridge
sagged in great gray waves

under the weight of someone else's past.
Tall ships of cloud massed of an afternoon.
Over the chalky cake of a college chapel,

they unfurled gray sail. In stained glass,
Saint Paul was rowed toward such a vessel
as once brought Pocahontas to this most British isle.

Married to a white man, presented to a king,
treated like a queen, she would be kept waiting
only for a wind to bear her home.

In Gravesend she would die of a white disease:
that, I had found, was where the West started
in the encyclopedia—in the estuary

of the Thames. At the next desk
a man slept facedown on an open book.
Oh, to lay my face like that to the page!

SWANS IN THE BASEMENT

On the edge of a dark mirror,
on the edge of a body of water—
in the hide I sat, and then, from the dark fen,

came swans from Iceland, swans from Siberia.
Like jets coming in, they banked,
the great webbed feet breaking the black glass.

Then they were galleons, they were caravels,
a ghost armada that noisily roiled, rocked,
and righted itself, each ship of feathers

shaken until it was watertight.
Like ballerinas, they preened and whined.
Like family, they nipped whoever came too close.

Over that mirror lying on its back,
open to the sky, let me button a long coat.
Keep it warm enough not to freeze,

not tonight, for, in back of that vast dark,
a white room opens. Once we were swans,
sister—do you remember?

In the desert, in the basement
of a house near the river, home of the ballet teacher.
Had we ever seen a swan? We learned

the French for climbing into the air.
We learned that a Russian master
needed just four words to make a dancer:

"Don't fall," he'd say, and then, "Get up."
Upstairs, something cooked slowly, sadly,
some secret recipe for disappointment.

Mrs. W. lavished no more words on us;
Mr. W. was home. He took off his dosimeter.
The sky yawned, emptier than ever.

The river waved its vacant blue
as if we were missing from it. I shook my head,
letting down my hair, a girl on the edge

of a mirror, the edge of a body of water
too small for a swan to take flight from,
though I didn't know that yet.

AT THE BEST OF TIMES

I

It was the best of times, it was the worst.
Was it the age of wisdom or of foolishness?
It was ninth grade, and we were reading Dickens.

We were going to heaven one day. We were going
the other way, or so our English teacher claimed.
She read us poetry. She read the newspaper.

Had a wall been built across Berlin?
An airplane been lost over Laos? Would a dam
on the Nile drown a long-lost dynasty?

A tavern too close to the Columbia River had flooded.
The Pasco-Kennewick-Richland *Tri-City Herald*
said the latest rage in Seattle had crossed the mountains,

forded the river, and arrived at the only nightclub
Richland had: an ax had been taken to a piano,
the remains forced down a hole in the floor.

Children of nuclear engineers, in the cyclotron
of the sixties, what were we hurtling toward?
Graduation was three long years away.

Who among us then would recall that old man
in a stagecoach on the London road?
He lowered the window, as if to look at us.

"Eighteen years!" said the passenger,
looking at the sun. "Gracious creator of day!
To be buried alive for eighteen years!"

II

It was the age of x, it was the age of y.
In Algebra, we were ruled by the golf coach
of Chief Joseph Junior High. In the sand

of a story problem, we flailed. Loving parabolas,
he perfected his swing. Adoring those curves
that came close enough to touch the axis

but then sailed on, he hit a ball, invisible,
over our heads and through the back wall.
Do I make him more interesting than he was?

He pursed his mouth into a zero.
His suits were gray as gravel.
As we counted the minutes left till lunch

one day in November, he would announce
the president was dead. But it was September
and we were leaving school early

to see Kennedy out in the desert.
He wore the hard hat he'd been given.
He waved a wand vaguely at our newest reactor.

How young we all were, fissile in the fierce sun.
It was over. Nothing to see, the crowd as spent
as uranium by the chain reaction of history.

THE GEOGRAPHY OF DREAM

Bumper to bumper, the nuclear chemists
crawled home from work, but my father
was no longer among them. In retirement,
he sat on his patio, flaking an arrowhead.

My old street, back in the Stone Age!
My soul, I left you there, explaining yourself
to a friendly mosquito. Once a week
a truck drove by, spraying something

that smelled of death on a summer evening.
Boys rode their bikes in its sour-sweet fog,
away from their mothers calling forlornly,
furiously calling. How did I come

to stand on the steps of a church long torn down,
at the feet of my eighth-grade teacher?
Sister Martin Mary wore the old habit,
the one I thought she'd abandoned.

Yards of black serge swathed all but her face,
as if she had no need of a body.
"Why have you come back?" she asked.
"I dismissed you ages ago."

Someone I no longer was sat on the ugly couch
in my parents' living room, waiting to give
the performance of her life. The front door was open,
cottonwoods murmuring. *Listen,* they said.

Don't listen to us. We're stuck here. Give us a drink.

LA PUSH

In from the ocean rushed a breeze
that didn't know its own strength
till it hit a huge cedar,

which gave a thirty-foot sigh but stood its ground.
Up to his ankles in the last of a wave,
a man of the tribe whose reservation this was

hauled in a hand-net. It glittered,
full of nothing but the small change
flung down by the late afternoon sun.

In the general store, the broken freezer
had been stocked with secondhand paperbacks.
Down the street, the Shaker chapel was open—

in the hollow heart of La Push,
I swam in the oily light and stink
of a penitential coat of paint. I sat

in a shipwreck of a chair and listened
to the surf pound a sermon into the shore,
whose sins were numberless as sand.

The sad psalms of seaweed were sung—
no, strung out to dry. The tide turned on itself.
Salvation reeked of sea wrack.

Nothing would bring the fish back
to La Push, back to the tribe,
not in that year of El Niño.

THE DESERT OF MEMORY

So he'd moved back home. Heavier,
somehow dulled—where was the pretty boy
who'd gone off to make movies years ago?

He sat on the homely couch in my parents' house.
His high school sweetheart had turned
into an expert on some voracious beetle.

Had we almost known each other once?
We seemed to know each other too well now.
The leaves of the cottonwood shivered

at the ghost of a wind. In the desert of memory,
downstream from the burial garden of nuclear waste,
the trees were bigger than I remembered,

afternoons longer, shadows deeper.
Did I once have a crush on that boy?
In the antechamber of a pharaonic tomb—

my parents' living room—a doctor's son
and a radiation monitor's daughter sat:
two clay figures, we'd been made over,

smaller than the classmates already gone
to the afterworld across the river,
where sprinklers labored in vineyards

ashimmer with disenchantment.
A hard Nilotic light anointed what lay within reach.
Don't move, the dust said, and then moved on.

SCHOLAR IN A NARROW STREET

after Tso Ssu

A pigeon beat its wings against a window.
A student in a narrow street
clasped her shadow, dragging her feet
through fallen leaves. She'd forgotten her book.

There was nowhere for her to go in all of Iowa
but the classroom, the empty desk in the front row.
She had composed an elegy
in the style of the ancient Chinese masters,

without knowing their language,
instead of writing the paper on . . .
well, she couldn't remember. O Tso Ssu!
Like your memorial, hers would be rejected.

She gasped, a carp in a pond gone dry.
Her father would suggest she turn her hand
to historical fiction. O bad novels of the bicentennial!
Hers went unwritten, for which give thanks.

For she would have failed to create a scholar
of Chinese poetry who, fleeing untranslatable terrors,
washed ashore on the banks of the Iowa River.
Did a hard inscrutable rain fall on a man

in a cape of reeds? The scholar erased a blizzard
of characters from the blackboard.
We started at dawn from the island of orchids, he sang
in his three-piece suit, his voice echoing from the chalk cliff.

Somewhere a water clock dripped. *I turn my head,*
an exile of the third century wrote, *and it seems only a dream
that I ever lived in the streets of Hsien-yang.*

LETTER OVER A THOUSAND YEARS LATE

Li Po, are you still drunk after all these years?
Tell me, which of us had the best moon in a poem?
For didn't every poem need one in those days?
The real moon swam the Iowa River to get away.

For nights were as dark as the fields on the edge of town,
blank pages already turned. Light-years away,
milk spilled: stars you couldn't see from a city
drifted closer together—or was it farther apart?

And with what coin we had, some bought song and drink,
and were drunk for months, scorning whatever there was
to scorn: the pigs, fellow poets, the endless corn.
Poetry, on the other hand, could lie like the president,

whose men had broken into a building with a name
that would never be beautiful again. O Watergate!
Master, tell me again: when an emperor is forced
to flee the palace, ought a poet compose a poem

to praise his ruler's "tour of the West"?
That fall, as if out of one of your scrolls,
there wandered into Iowa City a deer.
In the philosophy building, it climbed the stairs

as if they were the mountains missing from the Midwest.
On the top floor it fought to the death
its own reflection in a plate-glass window.
In a room lit by snow, I unbuttoned my shirt

for a man—but that is all I will tell you.

CHEKHOV FOR CHILDREN

She was in mourning for her life,
Masha loved to announce,
borrowing a line from another play.
With a swirl of black skirt,
she'd hurl herself into the arms
of an overstuffed chair in the dressing room.

Was it a line you had to be too young to say?
Who knew we'd never hear of that actress again,
who wore out a handkerchief in her grief?
I was handed a wad of shredded silk—
I the fourth sister, the one in the black
of a stagehand. Behind a folding screen,

waiting for Olga—the one who taught school—
I hid. Out of a corset and into a nightgown
I helped her change, as if into spinsterhood,
without missing her cue. There might be a fire
burning in town—she'd call that peace,
for want of a better word. O Iowa City,

Athens of the cornfields! Those sisters
stuck in the provinces pined for Moscow
as if for New York, or at least Chicago.
Perhaps even Cedar Rapids, with its tiny airport,
would do. Me—I'd never been so far east before.
I stood in the wings, waiting, I thought,

to relieve the colonel of a greatcoat as heavy
as his marriage. All he wanted
was to philosophize about the future,
but he was about to be ambushed by love.
A freight train whistled as it cut through campus,
bearing a sudden chill:

backstage a door had been stealthily opened—
and there lay the present, painted out in our absence.
Nothing moved in the whitened night
but a sisterly fury of snowflakes,
crystal snagging on crystal as they fell.

POETS AT FIFTY

In his first tuxedo,
a boy wrestled the womanly curves
of a bass viol up the steps to the music school.

Yes, I did. No, I didn't:
a katydid bowed the same note
as all the pale green, leaf-shaped others.

An "S" of garter snake
hugged the middle of the road,
in search of some last warmth, and wouldn't budge.

Over the lawns of Sewanee,
around the deer raiding flowerbeds,
fireflies signaled nothing but a male in search of a mate.

Who would say,
of that low, fitful light, that it was
not the more beautiful for fading so fast?

"Look at these beds,"
the ex-poet laureate said. "Sandstone
laid so flat, the last million years must have been dull."

In the twilight
of Tennessee, it was not the heat
so much as the humility: the smallest butterfly

in North America
closed the pages of its tiny book,
pages still a bluish blank, against the dark.

THE SECRET OF LANDSCAPE

Distant men have no eyes; distant trees have no branches.
Distant mountains have no stones, and yet they are as fine
and delicate as eyebrows. Distant water has no ripples,
and reaches up to the clouds. These are the secrets.

—WANG WEI

His head turned a little, as if toward the ghosts
of his old students. Facing the hill
to which his house clung, he pointed to a tree.
The body of the master might be wasting with age,

but I watched the tree at which he pointed
to see if a leaf moved, then looked away,
for didn't the true meaning of an object lie
in its shadow? Wasn't a figure, when seated,

only one seventh of an inch tall,
though its shadow might grow? The hills
of Iowa might appear higher than they ever were,
but the farther off an object, the smaller it became.

I spread a clean sheet of paper by the ink.
Even the highest hill filled just a square inch.
My first horizontal stroke covered a hundred miles.
Where was a bird to occupy such sky?

A POET DYING YOUNG

after Chang Tsai
in memory of John Bowie

When I was alive, I wandered the streets
of the old state capital, but now that I'm dead,
I lie in a cornfield outside of town. In the morning

of my life, how was I to know it was late afternoon?
I rose late. I read the student newspaper:
the weather report I'd written was my little fiction.

When the sun, red-eyed, had sunk
to the level of a Coralville motel,
I hung up my chariot and let the horses rest.

In the evening, could I be found in a booth
at the Deadwood? I don't remember.
Now not even you, my old classmates,

could make me age, though hair and teeth fall away
from us all. Not even those of you
who are still poets can escape this thing.

Beyond the world, I pull the rope
of the door tighter. I stuff my mouth
with ferns and roots as if with meat.

WRITER-IN-RESIDENCE IN LIMBO

after Li Po

How little they cared the cost!
Fine food on dishes of green jade,
like Ming grave goods—

if I had died and gone to heaven,
heaven was a minor outpost
far from the emperor's favor.

It was the raisin capital of the world,
where I ate and drank and did not think once
of you back east. I must have died.

One of the women drove me east
to see the giant sequoias. I was so small,
just clay in the shape of a servant at their feet;

far above me, boughs swished and sighed
like the silken sleeves of court,
the needles unthreading.

Sometimes we took boys with us
to carry the trappings of office,
giving ourselves up to the moment,

forgetting a semester was an eternity
and we were stuck with them. Still, their faces
were never smoother than in the chilly mirror

of that river. Even I grew younger.
Someone had brought a radio.
A thin wind blew cheap music into the dark

like cigarette smoke. O lost civilization!
Someone laughed at a splash,
or I heard a loon . . . but I must call a boy

and make him kneel before me
to tie this up. Love, there's a leaf
in the shape of a hand in this limbo

that I would send you, dark red,
and one like a waxy green heart.
There is much I have not told you.

IV

In 1776, between voyages to the Pacific, Captain James Cook dined with James Boswell in London. The next day, Boswell told Samuel Johnson that he wanted to accompany Cook on his next adventure. "One is carried away," Boswell said, "with the general, grand, and indistinct notion of a voyage round the world. "

Dr. Johnson deflated his companion's enthusiasm—"A man is to guard himself against taking a thing in general"—and Boswell stayed home.

—TONY HORWITZ

SOUTHERN ALTARPIECE

I. Good Friday

Here was the harrowing of hell:
in Starke, Good Friday noon.

The light was separated from the dark:
in the bakery, men made of gingerbread

or sugar-cookie dough lay on separate trays,
this being the South. Pink smiles wavered.

Blue buttons staggered down flattened chests.
Whose shaky hand had frosted them?

Someone in a rush to leave a place so hot
there were no flies? There were no customers,

either, for the cobbles of coffee cake.
On the hill of hot cross buns, sugary crosses slumped.

On the top shelf, brides and grooms stood stiffly,
faces pale, as if afraid they'd meet on a cake.

Past storks with babies in their beaks, past palm trees
of plastic, the couples gazed, not on each other,

but on the empty parking lot of eternity.

*

Through a hole in the wall of the bakery from hell,
I stepped into a store of dollhouse parts.

The air grew closer, as if this were the antechamber
of some great tomb for a king made god.

A newspaper the size of a postage stamp
seemed about to combust in the heat,

for the dead would have no use for news.
Fruit spun of glass, clay cakes, a plaster pie,

a jar of indigestion tablets: the votive offerings
had been laid out, shelf upon dusty shelf.

Pillars of an antebellum mansion lay on their sides.
The South would rise again, in miniature,

but for the fact there was nothing for sale
with which to make slave quarters behind the big house.

But there were toy bellows to raise a favorable wind
for a ship from Africa with a mortal cargo.

II. Holy Saturday

Outside the Church of Christ Lakefront,
the South smelled of old English churches

where prayers against mildew and rot
had gone unanswered. I drew in the awful incense

and held my breath as a one-legged bird appeared,
hopping the mudflats, almost keeping abreast

of the two-legged ones in its loose flock:
a lesser yellowlegs, according to the book.

Or a least yellowleg? A choir of cormorants moaned,
monks at matins. Like old air-conditioners,

they rattled, trying to cool this circle of hell.
Theirs was neither a waterlogged penitence

for not being oily or more reptilian,
nor some dark-feathered praise of the heavy air.

Another angel plunged into the wet, decomposing world,
then spread dark wings like laundry to dry.

*

So why was I standing on one leg at a traffic light?
There was no traffic that wilting afternoon,

yet suddenly a man appeared beside me.
"You're beautiful," he said. I looked around.

"I mean you no harm," he said, and stepped back.
Sunlight glanced off his gold eyetooth.

"The Book says to praise beauty where you see it."
"You're beautiful, too," I said. He looked down

at his denim vest, his bare chest. "No,
but tomorrow I will be," he said, as if by dawn

this angel the color of Easter chocolate
might guard the entrance of an empty tomb.

He extended his hand, dripping with rings.
What could I do but offer my plain one?

The light hadn't changed. And so it came to pass
that my hand was kissed by some stranger

one Holy Saturday somewhere south
of the end of the second millennium.

III. Easter Sunday

That Easter morning, what had risen?
Only an anole was to be found,

basking as if on a stone rolled back from a tomb.
Its back was striped with darkest lightning.

It waited to warm up enough to move.
I knew the feeling. I sat beside it on the front step

and tried not to breathe too hard. And so it was
I heard, on the faintest breeze, the only human sound:

a male voice from afar, not happy about something
and taking pains to make that clear,

though no consonants carried to the old porch
where we two creatures sat. Just the vowels

of fire and brimstone from the tent revival
on the edge of town, singed with jasmine and magnolia.

TO A LAKE DRYING UP

on my birthday

How long was the lake for this world?
From dock and bait shack it drew back,
stranding fish in pickerel weed,

to the delight of great blue herons
in ever greater number. Supermodels
on stilettos in the mud, they posed,

not bothering to feed, the feeding so good.
From the mouth of one beauty
came an ugly croak. A sodden logjam

of alligators digested this, not moved to move.
Gone the rowers who raced the dawn
in their sculls, and the fishers of dusk,

just birder and truant left wading the muck.
Then lake and I had the sky to ourselves
at last, a bowl empty even of cloud,

for this was Florida, where all weather is good
and that has to be good enough.
I was half a century old. Downshore

a woman my age viewed this
through binoculars: a body of water
dying even as it was born.

THE LOST HERODOTUS

Here men pass their lives
separate from the animals they eat.
They do not knead dough
with their feet or take up dung with their hands.

Every day they bathe
standing up and put on garments bearing names
of the small gods
who made their clothes. These people like to eat

in the out-of-doors
but relieve themselves in the house in secret.
After they drink
from metal beakers decorated with words,

these are collected
by a cart that requires not a single ox,
for burial at a special site,
for these people are mound-builders.

They leave their houses
to find cattle and chickens slaughtered,
and not by slaves.
And yet their buildings have reached the sky.

Their Parthenon I have seen,
farther away than any map could imagine.
The priest I asked
did not know when it was built.

Birds have been seen
to couple in the sacred precinct, so the gods
must be pleased.
Yet do these people have no great poet?

SUBTROPICAL APOCRYPHA

I. A Whooping Crane

had been sighted near St. Augustine.
     Hand-reared, escaped
from a small flock of birds nearly extinct,
     only to be shot—

in this lost book of the Apocrypha,
     it was hunting season
in the swamp. A ragged raft adrift in what
     was left of the lake

was just a thousand green-winged teal,
     asleep. From the far bank
came a rifle's report, understated and remote.
     And then, in the next chapter,

three men came toward me. They had no fish.
     They had no fishing poles.
The air thickened until I needed a knife
     to cut my way through it.

Flightless, I clutched a fat new field-guide
     of North American birds
to my featherless breast. A snakebird moaned.
     The lake went on dying,

as did something else—the sole catch of the day,
     dragged to the woods
by a vulture, only the underbelly eaten.
     Under a fish hook of moon,

an osprey skimmed the skin of the water
     and came up empty-clawed.

II. The Stranger

at the lake,
duck hunter, not bird-watcher,
        had better binoculars
than mine. He scanned the shallows.

Big and easy
were the birds I knew. But the small ones
        dark and low
in the water, just barely afloat,

a great raft of them?
"Blue-winged teal," he said, "A few hundred,
        asleep." I'd take his word,
though it proved wrong. I'd open my book

to what little I knew
of the hierarchy of herons: great blues,
        black-crowned nights,
tricolors, little blues and greens.

All wing and claw,
a hawk soared across the cover
        of the guidebook,
as if searching for food that moved.

"Once a live black chicken
fell out of the sky," the stranger said,
        "a mad kettle of feathers,
into my backyard." He lived in the country;

his nearest neighbor
had a chicken coop. Wings so wide,
        claws that clenched—a hawk
could have lifted a hen and flown for home,

until the burden
of argument became too much to bear.
And so it became,
for want of a better word, a gift,

one stranger to another.

BEAUTY IN FLORIDA

I. Beauty at Fifteen

We were too late to catch the moon,
already hauled from the swamp
and hung up to dry. Moon-melon,

new penny—I turned my back on it
and went on reading, for I was spleenful and fifteen.
I'd walked the wall I was sitting on now,

testing my balance on the distance
between my parents, which seemed to grow
with each wobble and flap of the arms.

Was my father king of less and less
as I grew older? Mother was queen
of the binoculars. A girl wants to be

a princess for Halloween, I announced.
Absently, some palm fronds clapped
from a great height, almost in the dark.

And I surprised a wood rat in a hurry.
But he was no footman in waiting,
not in the story whose pages I turned.

Down the highway, in the houses of men,
lights too low to be stars refused to move.
In such a palace, a girl might be well advised

to fall asleep for a hundred years.
I'd cover you in no time, the kudzu said
to no one in particular.

II. Beauty at Fifty

A path rose and sank as if with breath
through the swamp of dream.
It may or may not have crossed a tree trunk,

fallen, the last of some lost forest.
Where was the battlement of briars
the man who woke me said he'd come to?

Nothing was willing to snag our clothes.
Only a ground mist coiled as if to spring
and then unwound to let us through.

What was that pounding—rain on a road
somewhere near, or my heart in its cage?
I thought I saw something I recognized:

the town I grew up in, gathering dust.
Was it deserted? Houses kept their doors closed.
But then we were inside one, longing

not to be discovered before I found the way out.
I opened a door. There crouched the bedroom
of the girl I once was. A suitcase lay open

on the narrow bed, nothing packed but dust.
To my old kingdom a rat now laid claim,
though I had gone nowhere in all those years.

MISSING

I. Not There

There was no one in the house I'd borrowed
except the twilight of far-off Florida—

that purple you don't see anywhere else,
and then it's gone. Where were you?

There was no one, only night at the window,
the shade undrawn. A moth opened its book

to the same dusty page as always. What
was about to happen? Close the book!

A ghost of the subtropics, a pale pink gecko,
was looking up the word for food.

Through its skin, I saw a small blue heart.
Twin sacs of blue air emptied and filled.

The headlights of a car saw through it
and swept the room: no one was there.

No frog barked from a tree in the afterglow
of a thundershower. Love, remember

that student of ours whose boyfriend came
from the desert to visit? She said she woke one night

to find the door of the apartment open.
He was standing there, watching rain fall

in that relaxed and ruthless way it does.
Though she would marry and divorce him later,

in sleep she'd missed him, while he'd been missing
the kind of rain he'd never known.

II. Not Here

You weren't here. We didn't breathe the same air.
Mine held a note of smoke, as if prunings burned

in the vineyards. Or had the foothills turned to flame?
Outside my window—no, much farther off,

your absence rose like some foreign city.
It stood in water, admiring its reflection,

even in decay. Like you, it hadn't slept yet,
though its barges bore the burdens of a new day

past the old customhouse and the church
of Santa Maria della Salute: Venice needed Coke

and Xerox machines. And stacks of artichokes—
or at least their hearts afloat in lemon juice

so they wouldn't darken, exposed to the air.
I didn't know I could love a city the way I loved you.

A dredge scooped up mud for breakfast,
but Venice wouldn't wake from its dream of water.

A water taxi opened the Grand Canal like a book.
Its pages were green, edges deckled with foam.

In every slip and slap I read the long marriage
of city to lagoon. Each watery, salty kiss devoured.

How far away you were: I wrote zero after zero
down a page of the deepest green water.

THE MARRIAGE OF ORPHEUS

Something brushed my cheek with damp—
a leaf, its little valley slick with runoff

after rain. One last drop shook loose
and struck a spiderweb, which shuddered,

shuddered but cleaved to this grievous world
so a butterfly—a mourning cloak?—

could uncoil its watch spring of a tongue
in the time it took a limousine to stretch

down the thin twig of street, almost to my door.
Like a long albino snake gone straight,

tied with a big white bow—oh, pet,
you weren't mine. You belonged a few doors down—

here came a man in gold morning-coat,
carrying pale pink roses like a lute.

He leaned inside the dark cave of a car
to kiss someone I never saw, someone who reached out

and straightened his pink cravat.
Orpheus, would love turn back while it could?

Around the corner a nurse in white
stood at an open door, lifting her white arm

gently to bar the way of an old woman
bundled in hat and coat, though it was August.

"You don't have a daughter down the road,"
Persephone said to Eurydice. "You have no husband."

DEATH COMES TO FLORIDA

in memory of Donald Justice

I. The Pencil Museum of Cedar Key

One horseshoe crab lay against another,
    two antediluvian wheelbarrows,
        overturned. No, chariots
           abandoned

by the sea's retreat—and about to mate.
    "Can't you see they're busy?"
        I said. Nothing moved.
           The tide had turned

its back, and we—we were late for lunch
    with an old professor who was escaping
        the snow of Waterloo, Iowa.
           Out of the drifts

of a book he'd found in the little library,
    he told us the news. Which was
        all about Napoleon,
           that hermit crab

who didn't yet know his last empty shell
    of a home would be found on an island
        bigger than this one
           but even more remote.

The old poet's voice was a ghost of itself.
    The fish of the day, he whispered—
        though we were the only ones
           in the restaurant—

was the same as yesterday. Over the worn keel
　　　of his shoulder, I saw pelicans
　　　　　lumber in from the Gulf
　　　　　　like jumbo jets

and land on the roof of a shack that shook
　　　but managed to hold a little longer.
　　　　　Where were the cedars
　　　　　　of Cedar Key?

In the end, we didn't go to the museum.
　　　The great age of the pencil had come
　　　　　and gone, word by word,
　　　　　　tree by tree.

II. Last Winter

He was not himself. He was just a shell
    a hermit crab had made into home
       a while, then left behind.
          In Cedar Key

that February, he sat in the tide of talk
    that lapped around him, listening.
       What did he hear
          that we could not?

Some great storm whiting out his years
    in Iowa, then Florida as well?
       Out the picture window
          he kept his back to,

a fog refused to lift from a gulf it painted
    as gray as itself. We drove home
       in the dark, on highway
          straight and empty.

So very deep the dark—suddenly you swerved:
    we'd nearly hit something just beyond
       the reach of the headlights.
          Something as dark

as the night and almost as big, crossing as if
    it owned this neck of the swamp:
       a wild boar from an engraving
          by Dürer, who had cast it

not as Death but as the Devil. Yet how noble
    in bearing, that dark rumble of cloud,
       shaggily trotting on cloven hoofs
          as if wearing high heels.

It crashed into a thicket of cross-hatching.
Somewhere a knight rode on, sure
Death was an old man on foot
waving an hourglass,
easily outrun.

III. Orpheus in Florida

Tongue by white tongue, petal by petal,
    spring lay where it had fallen,
        though it was only February.
            Still, this was Florida.

Down the road from the River Styx,
    a ditch held dirty water—
        and something else,
            something

a clot of vultures didn't want me to see.
    Their priestly robes fluttered,
        wings hunched in prayer,
            beaks ready to feast

upon death as soon as I said a word
    over—what? A dog? A deer?
        The skull was skinned,
            bone licked smooth.

Unfathomable the empty pool of the eye
    that refused to meet my gaze.
        From the dark heart
            of the woods,

a single note tolled, like breaking glass:
    a wren with feathers the color of dirt
        tossed aside by the spade
            of a gravedigger

warned the shades of my presence,
    I who would sing the dead,
        though they turn me away
            when I draw near.

IV. An Elegy Prepares Itself

after Yuan Mei, 1795

Like a god with another world to create,
    you get up even earlier when you're old.
        No one else is around.
            No kitchen-smoke rises.

You want to wash, but no water's been heated.
    You want a drink, but no tea's been made.
        You want to shout but remember
            the old days,

when you, too, lay abed. Where was I going?
    I can't remember. If I step into the garden,
        the earth reaches up to welcome me.
            If I dare climb the stairs,

the house panics. By the time you arrive
    at my grave, I will have forgotten you.
        Sit with me till the third watch.
            Tell me why you're here.

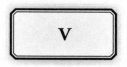

V

Reader, why hast thou been spared?
To what purpose hast thou been left till now?

—ST. PETER'S CHURCH,
UPWELL, ENGLAND

TO A SEA-UNICORN

In Paris once,
where these things can happen,
across the street from the Louvre, I came
to a stand of walking sticks.
Against the window

of an antique shop,
they leaned like bare trees
in the Tuileries, as if to get out of the wind,
though they were indoors.
I knew the feeling.

I drew my coat closer
against the Napoleonic cold.
The canes swaggered no more. Out on their own,
they'd taken a wrong turn
from the past,

only to find
their walking days over.
The one with a cut-glass knob, the silver-handled,
and the one with a snake turning back
on itself: in their midst,

towering over them,
a narwhal tusk as tall as I was—
like the one I'd seen in a room where it was still
the fifteenth century. Where,
in the unicorn tapestries,

only the lady aged,
panel by panel, until she and I
were of an age too old to countenance a unicorn,
no matter how handsome.
Narwhal, sea-unicorn,

your four-footed,
goat-bearded ghost no longer walks
this earth, avoiding capture except by the artist.
Its horn no longer parts the folds
of a maiden's skirt.

Is this enough
to save you, my unlikely one?
The ocean of the north is yours, as it always was.
The ice spreads a blanket over it.
Water falls on water,

mille fleurs of snow
through which you surface in air
cold enough to carve, a whale with a tooth
that spirals into a tusk of dream—
no one knows why.

REST ON THE FLIGHT INTO EGYPT

And so to the fifteenth century, in a far corner of the Louvre—
where, when Madonna and Child stopped to rest

on the flight into Egypt, they found themselves
in the Netherlands. How languid they were,

as if too well-born to require bones.
Two angels were needed to lift the blue

of the Virgin's train above the Dutch dirt.
And yet a fisherman noticed nothing

but the lack of fish in a greenish lake.
Had the donkey refusing to budge

seen something besides the swan gliding away
from *le Maître aux Cygnes* (as the painter,

whose name has been lost, is known)?
In vain the beast's owner held up a cudgel

to the blue velvet of heaven. Would he be struck
by one of the thin gold rays that fell from on high

indiscriminately? Something had stunted the trees
over which even the Child towered.

Nothing cast a shadow yet in Western art;
there was no shade to be had, or need of it.

ON THE FEAST OF THE INNOCENTS

Where were we? In the Métro,
somewhere under Paris. A chill December,

and the scruffily seraphic boy across the aisle
was bored. All he had to play with

was a pen, no paper, his fingers bloody with red ink.
His mother wanted to sleep.

She held out her hand, which he turned over,
and on the tired skin he drew—what was it?

Something almost Euclidean,
hair spiraling out from a round, flat face

balanced on an almost equilateral dress.
"Une femme?" she asked. "Un ange," he said,

in the season when wings might be mistaken
for the puffy sleeves of a party gown.

And, if this weren't enough to deliver them,
next to the angel he drew an automobile aslant,

long and low and trailing flames, it could go so fast.
Child, where would you go? You won't remember this,

which is as it should be. Let your mother sleep.
Let no harm come to you in her dream.

PARIS IN THE ICE AGE

In the Luxembourg Gardens, all that stirred
was a jogger pushing a little cloud of breath
up the stone stairs, and a lone gardener.

But in winter's kingdom, what was left
for him to do? He searched in vain
for one last twig to prune. Did a curtain quiver

at an upper window of the long, blond palace
of Marie de' Medici? From the height
at which a knot garden was best viewed,

the ghost of a queen looked down
on a Tuscany still carved from the Latin Quarter.
Where was a nursemaid to push a pram

that would bob on the gravel path like a boat?
Where was a boy to sail a tall toy ship
to the farthest shore of the man-made pond?

It was not the season. The baroque fountain
of the dead queen had frozen: gulls walked the ice
toward something small and fleshy.

Torn open like the wax seal on a lost last letter
from her weak son the king—in death she'd return
to watch the gulls feed on one of their own.

PARIS, CITY OF THE DEAD

I

Later, the day turned cold, too cold for snow.
In the hard winter light below Montmartre,
an angel of darkness appeared:

Sunday afternoon on the Place Pigalle,
a woman clad in scraps of black leather
towered above me, bending as low

as her stilettos allowed. It was nothing personal.
What good to her now was Toulouse-Lautrec
known in the brothels of Paris as "The Coffeepot"?

What good Degas and the dancing girls he chalked?
The dead weren't much of an audience,
so she stalked the living. Across from the Sexodrome,

she laid her hand lightly on my shoulder
and promised the two of us something
my high school French class hadn't covered.

II

It was all downhill from Montmartre.
The street became a bridge over a city
of the dead within the city of light.

In that underworld beneath an overpass,
small stone houses lined cobbled streets
just wide enough for a hearse.

The lanes bore their names on signs
so the living wouldn't get lost—
and yet we took a wrong turn

on the way from Nijinsky to Truffaut.
Each house had a door for its front wall,
and sometimes, in the tiny room inside,

an old kitchen chair, so you could sit
and with a finger trace names and dates
carved to make wallpaper.

In the bare bones of the trees,
magpies rattled like professional mourners.
Ravens screamed that we weren't wanted.

A cat the dingy gray of the oldest tombs
slunk out from behind one, saw me, and turned
to stone. Even artificial flowers shivered.

Children deported fifty years ago,
there is a marker for you here,
where you never played. Your stone is still as clean

as if just washed with tears, starched, and ironed.
On it pebbles have been laid, as is the custom
of your people, though your ashes fell

somewhere else, unmarked, even colder.

THE PARAKEETS OF AMSTERDAM

A cage went in search of a bird.
—Franz Kafka

What was I longing for?
Something wavered. Was it me or the window
    of the Hotel Rembrandt?

We overlooked a canal where bales of cloud
    fell overboard from a sky
that rode low over land even lower.

    Thin houses knelt
by the shallow Calvinist waters.
    Love, where were you?

An ocean away across the room
    on the boat of a bed.
I wanted to say—but then I saw

    green feathers flying
down the wet street, a small formation
    so foreign in color

they had to be parakeets. Already
    it was too late to show you.
Love, those leafy, unlikely feathers!

    A long way
from the Himalayan foothills of home,
    that rose-ringed parakeet.

Which way was India? I cocked my head
    at the world below:
clipper ships of cloud capsized in the canal.

Leaf sawed across leaf.
What could I say? A door opened
in the cage of *paradijs*.

IN A LOW COUNTRY

I. In the Ocean

of an aquarium, fish came and went
while we sat and waited in a seafood restaurant.
The evening might have dragged its nets
through the dark canals of Amsterdam

to catch a moon as flat as a flounder,
but here the tropical fish were safe,
except from the hungers of one another.
Out from the lip of a rock, one shimmered.

A Dutch blonde out on a date in fur and pearls;
an Indonesian at work at a picture window
in the red-light district, wearing a whole lot less,
just a seaweed of lace—when our kind walked out

of the water onto the dirt, we lost all grace.
Except for the old man who worked his way
through a huge *plateau* of shellfish, tier by tier.
There was no shell he couldn't break into,

as if picking a lock, if he chose the right tool
from those the waitress had arrayed before him.
There was no wife to watch, just a fish,
a high hat rubbing its dorsal fin against the glass.

A yellow-lined sweetlips lost its stripes,
fading to the dull brown of an adult.
Like the croaker who gave the glass a kiss,
you were mouthing something in the din,

love, something I couldn't catch.

II. In the Desert

the sun, that fire god, was burning.
No wind dared lift a single grain of sand.
No one stepped forth from the tomb to scrub the stoop,
though this was Holland. In the museum,

a model city of the dead filled one room,
and down upon it a little spotlight shone.
But where was the antechamber swept clean
by the archaeologist so he could camp in comfort

while he read the walls? Where was the corner
in which he carved his name and the date?
Did he leave a tin of beans, a scrap of newspaper
among the ancient artifacts? For, though his brain

be unraveled by a curved copper hook,
his stomach stored in the canopic jar by his side,
he would need sustenance in the afterlife.
For he would have to reach the Field of Reeds,

where the afterworld would turn out to be as wet
as the Netherlands he'd left for the desert.
Where was there a drop of well water to purify myself,
though I was merely a tourist? In rivulets,

rain stormed the high windows of a lost Golden Age.
In Amsterdam it fell on an ice skate of bone
still buried, on dice made of knucklebones
lost in the dark of the deep blue mud.

THE LATER PORTRAITS

I. In Red Light

Like angels in old paintings, half there,
half not, women in their underwear

drifted into view. Like tropical fish
nosing up to the glass of an aquarium

lit with red light, at nine in the morning
they looked bored: round the dirty ribs

of the Oude Kerk, the footsteps on the cobbles
were worthless to them, being merely mine.

More anchoress than angel,
none of these women—not even the transvestite—

was white-skinned. Two centuries after it had died,
the Dutch East India Company lived on

behind the great whitewashed shell of a church
from which every angel had been stripped.

Remains of the old stained-glass had been rehung,
a few bright islands in a Pacific of blank panes.

II. In Stained Glass

Inside the old church, I stood in a puddle
of light that had fallen, sanguine,

from the scraps of a gown of glass.
I stood at the blushing door to the sacristy.

Locked. Could Saskia Uylenburgh,
promised to a painter beneath her station,

have read the words in soot and gold leaf
on the lintel? The thorns of old Dutch

scratched out *Marry in haste, repent at leisure.*
I stood on a stone in a vast North Sea

of church floor, beside a slab bearing her first name
and a date. Her husband would live on

till even his portraits had fallen out of fashion.
Apprentices long gone, he would pay to be rowed

to the field where a young murderess had been hanged,
her skirts tied shut to prevent further spectacle.

With a tenderness brutal from long practice,
he would draw her twice, on the best Japan paper.

III. In Light Rain

Not far from his old house in Amsterdam,
that Sunday morning, Rembrandt stood in the doorway

of Madame Tussaud's. He was shorter than I expected.
Did we see eye to eye? Not quite. He stood at an easel,

his brush lifted as if to catch a tear, a drop of rain—
anything to make a mark, however faint.

Who could afford to sit for him in death?
And where were the famous furs, the gold chains?

His robe, his paint rag, stirred in the wind.
Where was the Venetian mirror that had looked

so long and hard at him? He looked through me,
just a wet tourist on the Nieuwe Zijde.

He looked toward the Jordaan. Where was the girl
named Anne, who'd hidden in an attic during the war?

She would have been seventy-two this year.
Let the dead paint the dead.

THE DOLLHOUSES OF THE DEAD

I

To see the past better,
you had to climb a little ladder,
the Dutch dollhouse was so tall.
In the attic of the seventeenth century,

nothing dared be out of order;
four maids saw to that, the lady of the house
left standing by her bed, dressed in gold silk,
empty-handed. She wouldn't meet

the mirror's gaze. She couldn't be made to sit.
In the nursery next door, a tiny back was turned:
a child waiting to be fed, not by her mother,
but by a nurse hidden in shadow.

Or was she to be teased by her brother,
a gingerbread boy in velvet and lace?
There were linens to be pressed,
but not by him. The blankest of sheets,

they waited as if to be sewn into books.
History, you are rubbed with spices
from the Far East, just a basket
of game birds on their way to the spit.

II

Before she went into hiding,
did a Jewish girl named Anne stand
on those steps in the Rijksmuseum,
to see a normal day in 1690?

To see the past better,
I had to climb her steep Dutch stairs
to an attic stripped bare in 1944.
But first I looked down into a model of it.

As if a family of dolls—merchant and wife,
two teenage daughters—had just stepped out
for an afternoon: there, in miniature,
was what her father, who survived the war,

remembered. A scrap of ugly carpet.
A map the size of a postage stamp,
where red dots followed, like pinpricks of blood,
the tracks of the Allies from Normandy.

The pictures his youngest had cut from magazines
and pasted to the wall of her narrow room—
O dead starlets of the thirties,
may history be kind to you here.

A PEARL EARRING

Perhaps it was glass, a little globe
coated inside with a film of fish scales
by some clever, vulpine Venetian.
The young woman who wore it,

her mouth open to speak—
was she about to tell us that?
No, she looked across the room
in that house in The Hague.

She looked clear through us
to where there hung a view of Delft,
the only place she'd ever been.
She'd never seen a real pearl.

Every brick in the old town wall
had been blurred until beautiful,
monument to nothing more lasting
than mud. How many colors

to convince us each brick existed?
The wall was painted deep in shadow,
cast by the only Dutch mountains,
the wet dark clouds of history.

Would she say Vermeer had cheated
and moved a church steeple?
It wasn't the pink but a gray green
that gave the lie of life to her cheek.

WILLIAM THE SILENT

At the tomb of William the Silent,
I stood in silence. You, a much later William,
unrelated to the story, read aloud
that the king hadn't held his tongue so much
as kept his own counsel. He kept it still.

The New Church, in which we stood
and the dead king lay, hadn't been new for centuries.
The young tourist we'd passed outside,
leaning on a buttress, smoking a joint,
this being Holland—there was no sign of him.

Nor of the dog on the loose
who'd nosed into a butcher shop across the street
and been yelled at for his trouble—a dog
straight out of those old Dutch paintings
where, to the burghers and their wives

dwarfed by the bleak geometry of heaven
that was this whitewashed interior,
the painter had dared to add
an unholy hound morosely chasing its tail
around the dead tree trunk of a column.

No such creature ventured now to sniff
at the dog carved curled at his ruler's stone feet.
Did I believe the animal had died of grief?
I wanted to. I wanted to tell you that.
I wanted this to be a love poem,

if not, somehow, to you, then to the silence
submerged in the weak, watery light
that it had taken ages to enclose, then to drown.
Did the heavy marble robes guard against the chill?
The stone pillow seemed to give under the king's head.

AN EMPTY ROOM IN DELFT, WHERE A LINE OF MANDELSTAM'S IS FOUND

As if in a dream, I came to a black box
in the middle of the last room.
I looked inside, Carel Fabritius.
I looked back three centuries
at the even smaller room you'd painted there
painstakingly. Did you want me to?
Did the floor go up a wall? From one angle, yes.
A chair took on a third dimension
but stayed resolutely empty.
Sensing my eye as huge as a god's
at the peephole, someone had stepped
into one you never painted, leaving a door ajar.

Fabritius, was that room yours?
Your soul could rest there, if it crouched.
But the goldfinch you painted life-size
on a small canvas—the one chained to its perch,
trained to haul a small bucket of seed up from below—
would be too big. Dead man, don't worry
if you haven't seen that bird since the day
Delft went dark with flame, your last night
on the wet, flat earth of Holland. Someone unseen
holds out a mirror and some salve.
There's a toy boat with which to cross
the sunlight spilled on the floor.
Because the soul is fond of trifles.

A VIEW OF DELFT

I

The earth was flat and growing flatter:
I had seen it from the tower
of the old Nieuwe Kerk.
I had climbed a corkscrew to heaven,
clutching a handrail of old rope:
the earth was flat and wet,
and, clearly, it would be years
before, over the edge of the world,
a tiny ship would come, blue
with distance, riding a blue ruffle
of waves as if painted on a tile.

A ship that bore news of an island
bought for a few strings of beads—
New Amsterdam, you're no longer
an island of open fields.
Where is the wall of Wall Street?
What is a name but a ledger slab
of loss, laid in the floor of a church
to cover the bones of the dead?
What is history but these dates,
worn away underfoot,
until, its graves unmarked,
the Old World is like new?

II

O Delft! Where was the house
of Rembrandt's best pupil,
who'd died, too young, the night
the powder magazine exploded?
Long ago rebuilt. Wind off the polders
tried to sway the tower. And Vermeer's house?
Torn down to widen the street
for the age of the automobile.
Rain whipped again my American cheek.

On our way back to Earth,
we passed a room full of clockwork
just as it ratcheted to life,
each gilded gear bent on waking just enough
to make a bell mark an afternoon
no one would remember.
A wave of sound crashed through my body
as if it weren't there, holding its breath.
Through a slit in the stone
just wide enough for an archer's fist,
I could almost reach the hands of the clock,
huge, surprisingly feminine.
They almost touched.
It was the tenth of September
in the year of our Lord 2001.

ACKNOWLEDGMENTS

Agni: "Letter over a Thousand Years Late," "Nagasaki, 1600"

Antioch Review: "Poets at Fifty"

Gettysburg Review: "Paris, City of the Dead," "A Poet Dying Young," "Rest on the Flight into Egypt," "Southern Altarpiece"

Horace, The Odes: New Translations by Contemporary Poets, edited by J. D. McClatchy (Princeton University Press, 2002): "1.14," "2.36"

Literary Imagination: "An Elegy Prepares Itself," "A View of Delft"

Margie: "The Geography of Dream," "Letter Four Hundred Years Late"

The Nation: "The Marriage of Orpheus"

New Criterion: "Chekhov for Children," "On the Feast of the Innocents," "Taxi to Stonehenge," "Writer-in-Residence in Limbo"

New England Review: "The Desert of Memory," "Orpheus in Florida," "The Pencil Museum of Cedar Key," "To a Lake Drying Up"

Notre Dame Review: "The Coast of Bohemia," "Letter Two Hundred Years Late," "The Lost Herodotus," "Missing," "The Parakeets of Amsterdam"

Paris Review: "Beauty in Florida," "To the Fifties"

Poetry Northwest: "An Empty Room in Delft, Where a Line of Mandelstam's Is Found"

Raritan: "La Push," "The Secret of Landscape," "To a Sea-Unicorn"

Salmagundi: "At the Best of Times," "A Pearl Earring"

Sewanee Review: "The Dollhouses of the Dead," "The Giant Octopus of Puget Sound," "The Green Woodpecker," "To the Sixties," "To the Seventies," "On Storey's Way"

Shenandoah: "Paris in the Ice Age"

Smartish Pace: "Brighton, 1877," "In a Low Country"

Southern Review: "William the Silent"

Southwestern Review: "To the West"

Triquarterly: "Her Posthumous Life," "To the Eighties," "To the Nineties," "To the Double Oughts," "The Later Portraits," "Swans in the Basement"

Virginia Quarterly Review: "Scholar in a Narrow Street"

Yale Review: "Subtropical Apocrypha"

DEBORA GREGER is the author of seven previous books of poems, *Movable Islands*; *And*; *The 1002nd Night*; *Off-Season at the Edge of the World*; *Desert Fathers, Uranium Daughters*; *God*; and *Western Art*. She has won, among other honors, the Grolier Prize, the Discovery/*The Nation* Award, the Peter I. B. Lavan Younger Poets Award, an Award in Literature from the American Academy and Institute of Arts and Letters, and the Brandeis University Award in Poetry. She has received the Amy Lowell Poetry Travelling Scholarship and grants from the Ingram Merrill Foundation, the Guggenheim Foundation, and the National Endowment for the Arts. She lives in Florida and in Cambridge, England.

PENGUIN POETS